KU-473-317

Anxiety.

How to Calm Your Thoughts and Quieten Your Mind

Debbi Marco

ANXIETY

Copyright © Summersdale Publishers Ltd, 2020

All rights reserved.

No part of this book may be reproduced by any means, nor transmitted, nor translated into a machine language, without the written permission of the publishers.

Debbi Marco has asserted her moral right to be identified as the author of this work in accordance with sections 77 and 78 of the Copyright, Designs and Patents Act 1988.

Condition of Sale
This book is sold subject to the condition that it shall not, by way of trade or otherwise, be lent, resold, hired out or otherwise circulated in any form of binding or cover other than that in which it is published and without a similar condition including this condition being imposed on the subsequent purchaser.

An Hachette UK Company
www.hachette.co.uk

Vie Books, an imprint of Summersdale Publishers Ltd
Part of Octopus Publishing Group Limited
Carmelite House
50 Victoria Embankment
LONDON
EC4Y 0DZ
UK

www.summersdale.com

Printed and bound in the Czech Republic

ISBN: 978-1-78783-264-0

Substantial discounts on bulk quantities of Summersdale books are available to corporations, professional associations and other organizations. For details contact general enquiries: telephone: +44 (0) 1243 771107 or email: enquiries@summersdale.com.

Introduction

Most people experience some worry or fear around certain situations. It is perfectly natural to feel anxious before a job interview or when you are going through big life changes, but sometimes anxiety starts to creep into everyday situations such as going to work or seeing friends. It becomes a problem when your anxiety appears more regularly, lasts longer or becomes more extreme. If your anxiety is increasing to unhealthy levels, make sure you seek professional help. Often you can learn to manage your anxiety using some simple tricks and tips to train yourself to worry less. Here you will find some practical advice to lift your mood and calm your mind.

WHAT IS ANXIETY?

Anxiety is rooted in the "fight or flight" response and symptoms can include negative thoughts, overanalyzing conversations, insomnia, nausea, sweating or panic attacks. What causes your anxiety and how it manifests itself will be unique to you. This doesn't mean that what is worrying you is more or less serious than what might be worrying someone else, but it is important to take steps to address your worries before they get too serious – which is why reading this book is a great idea!

IDENTIFY YOUR FEARS

Sometimes anxiety can feel as though it is floating around your body for no discernible reason. Grab a piece of paper and write down everything that is bothering you, however small or silly those things might be. When everything is clearly laid out in black and white, you can start to understand what is niggling you and how you can make things better.

Seeing
the Signs

Not everybody who suffers from anxiety recognizes it. Perhaps you are very high functioning, or you don't display outward physical symptoms. Remember, even if you only check a few things on the list, you can still help yourself by practising self-care. Signs of anxiety include: difficulty controlling your worry, trouble sleeping, rapid breathing or a tight chest, regular feelings of panic and nervousness, and avoiding social situations. Seek help if your anxiety is causing you to feel depressed or have suicidal thoughts, or if it is affecting your relationship or job. Whatever your levels of anxiety, there is help out there for you. Just be brave and speak to someone you trust rather than suffering in silence – you may be surprised by how many people feel the same as you.

YOU MAY NOT
CONTROL ALL THE
EVENTS THAT HAPPEN
TO YOU, BUT YOU CAN
DECIDE NOT TO BE
REDUCED BY THEM.

Maya Angelou

**Once you choose hope,
anything's possible.**

Christopher Reeve

Be Honest

The first step in dealing with your anxiety is to own it. Admit to yourself that you are struggling and that things are hard right now. They won't always be this way, but you need to face up to what you are dealing with. Perhaps your anxiety is social, work related or to do with money. Whatever it is, take some time to sit quietly and think about your problems – you could write a list or draw a picture to represent what is going on with you at the moment.

It may feel overwhelming at first, but taking the time to really see what is going on in your life will help. You might make connections that weren't obvious. For example, perhaps you were worried about going to a party, but actually it is one individual who is the root of your concern. And don't forget, you won't feel like this forever – you will one day be able to overcome these feelings of anxiety.

You don't have to control your thoughts. You just have to stop letting them control you.

Dan Millman

DON'T PRETEND

Sometimes it feels like the easiest option is to pretend everything is fine and that you have all aspects of your life under control, but this could be adding to your anxiety. The pressure of keeping up the appearance that everything is okay could actually be making you feel worse. Pretending to be fine is draining, but if you start to be honest with yourself and others you'll find it easier to tackle the root of your problems.

KEEP IT REAL

It's easy to believe our negative thought patterns are the truth, but just because something might happen, it doesn't mean it definitely will. For example, if your bus breaks down on the way to work, you might start to worry about what will happen if you're late: perhaps your boss will call you in to their office and tell you off or you might be put on probation. When anxiety takes hold, it is easy to catastrophize and take any situation to its worst possible end. Try to break down your negative thoughts by asking yourself why this terrible thing might happen and then think of a more positive alternative. Of course, there's no guarantee the worst won't happen, but when you start to frame events with different possible scenarios and outcomes, it will seem much less likely. If you start to treat your negative thoughts like a feeling instead of the truth, you can begin to train yourself to move away from the worst-case scenario and see a different, less stressful possibility.

Our anxiety does not come from thinking about the future, but from wanting to control it.

Kahlil Gibran

BE YOUR OWN FRIEND

Imagine your buddy made a massive mistake at work and confided in you about it. Would you berate them and call them stupid? Would you tell them they will probably lose their job and that everyone thinks they're incompetent? Of course not, so why would you say it to yourself? Next time you start to beat yourself up internally, pause and imagine you're talking to a good friend instead. You'll find it easier to be kinder and more rational with a different perspective.

Say No to Negativity

Often there seems to be a voice inside us that exists just to point out the negatives. Maybe it says you won't do well at your job interview, that your banter isn't up to scratch or you look terrible in every outfit you try on. Identify this voice, thank it for its advice and shut it down. As you get more practised in ignoring your inner critic, it will appear less and less, leaving you more space for positive thoughts. Try labelling any negative thoughts you may have, such as when you are being overcritical or catastrophizing (thinking of the worst possible outcome) and put them in imaginary boxes in your head. This will help you recognize when you are being particularly tough on yourself and the mental act of filing away these thoughts will make it easier to not dwell on them.

I PROMISE YOU
NOTHING IS AS
CHAOTIC AS IT SEEMS...
NOTHING IS WORTH
POISONING YOURSELF
INTO STRESS, ANXIETY
AND FEAR.

Steve Maraboli

Nothing diminishes anxiety faster than action.

Walter Anderson

Take Some Time Out

If you're finding yourself stuck in a cycle of negativity, take time out and do something different. Try to avoid any triggers – such as social media or staying in bed for too long – and instead find something creative to do. You could upcycle a piece of furniture or go for a walk and photograph some nature, or bake a cake. Whatever you choose to do, make sure it's an activity you enjoy and not something you find end up feeling lower than before. By doing something creative your mind will have a renewed focus and will be forced to switch out of negative thought patterns. A change of scene or a change of perspective will help break your negative thoughts and set you on a more positive path. If you can find several things you find calming, you'll soon have a full toolbox you can turn to when you need to distract yourself from anxious thoughts.

**Don't go through life;
grow through life.**

Eric Butterworth

BE YOUR OWN JUDGE

It is easy to assume every negative thought we have is true, but the next time a negative thought pops into your head, put it on trial. What evidence do you have? Has anyone else said this to you? Ask yourself if there are any other possible truths on the matter and try to build up as many as you can. If you can start to recognize false thoughts and worries, you will start to take away their power over you.

IT'S OKAY TO BE SCARED. BEING SCARED MEANS YOU'RE ABOUT TO DO SOMETHING REALLY, REALLY BRAVE.

MANDY HALE

CONFIDE IN A FRIEND

One of the worst things about anxiety is feeling as though you're the only one who is struggling with it. Take the time to talk to a close friend or family member about how you're feeling. You might be surprised to discover they struggle with some of the same feelings and are able to be a reassuring presence, as well as offer practical support and suggestions.

THE GREATEST
WEAPON AGAINST
STRESS IS OUR
ABILITY TO CHOOSE
ONE THOUGHT
OVER ANOTHER.

William James

Present fears are less than horrible imaginings.

William Shakespeare

BREAKFAST MATTERS

You might only want a cup of coffee in the morning, but fuelling your body properly will help your mental health. Try to include a little protein to keep you fuller for longer and choose slow-releasing carbs such as porridge, a smoothie with oats or poached eggs on wholewheat toast. You'll find your energy levels and blood sugar will remain steady, leaving you free to face your day without the added stress of being hungry.

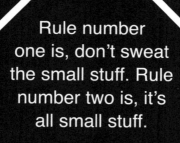

Rule number one is, don't sweat the small stuff. Rule number two is, it's all small stuff.

Robert Eliot

Eat the Rainbow

Your diet has a direct effect on your mood and ability to handle stress. If you are loading yourself with unhealthy food and an unvaried diet, it's no surprise your anxiety levels are creeping up. Instead nourish your body with balanced, healthy meals that incorporate a range of colours: fruits, vegetables and proteins such as fish or seeds and grains. By "eating the rainbow" you have a better chance of getting all the vitamins and nutrients you need to be happy and healthy. Best of all, you'll find your brain responds positively to a healthy, varied diet and you will have more energy for exercising and being productive. You don't have to spend hours preparing your meals, and simple tasks such as chopping vegetables or following a recipe have been found to be meditative, so you can nourish your body and calm your mind at the same time.

A crust eaten in peace is better than a banquet partaken in anxiety.

Aesop

Whatever is going to happen will happen, whether we worry or not.

Ana Monnar

Eat Mindfully

When you're feeling low it can be easy to bury your feelings by eating a tub of ice cream or piles of sweet treats. And while there's no reason for you not to have something sweet occasionally, be careful you're not comfort eating to deal with your emotions. If you feel you are struggling with disordered eating, ask for help from your doctor. But if you know you tend to rely on food to distract you from stress, try to change unhealthy snacks in the house and if you do feel like snacking, distract yourself by going for a walk or calling a friend. If you still really want to eat something unhealthy, try to eat only half your usual portion. If you can get a handle on your unhealthy snacking, it will feed positively into other aspects of your health, for example being able to exercise more and giving you the space to examine the parts of your life that are causing you anxiety.

HE WHO IS NOT
EVERY DAY
CONQUERING
SOME FEAR HAS
NOT LEARNED THE
SECRET OF LIFE.

SHANNON L. ALDER

STAY HYDRATED

Drinking enough water seems like an obvious thing to do, but very few people keep their hydration levels adequately topped up, especially when they are stressed and busy. Being dehydrated can have a very real effect on your mood and health. If you're dehydrated you can feel tired, foggy and unable to focus. If you struggle to remember to drink, invest in a smart bottle or set alerts on your phone that will send you gentle reminders to keep sipping throughout the day.

The man who removes a mountain begins by carrying away small stones.

Chinese proverb

Nothing is permanent in this wicked world – not even our troubles.

Charlie Chaplin

Think Before You Drink

Alcohol is a known depressant, so if you are dealing with stress by treating yourself to a glass of wine or a beer you might actually be making your anxiety worse. Try to build in alcohol-free days each week. Gradually build these up until you can go for a week or two without drinking. If you have a social engagement, try to stick to a limited number of drinks or make the decision not to drink at all. If you struggle to say no at social events, it's perfectly fine to assign yourself as designated driver or tell people you're taking antibiotics to avoid the peer pressure to drink, at least to begin with. Once you've proved to yourself you can have fun without drinking, it will be easier to do again. If you think you may have a problem with alcohol, don't be afraid to seek professional help.

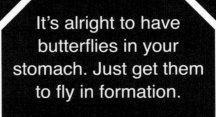

It's alright to have butterflies in your stomach. Just get them to fly in formation.

Rob Gilbert

The elimination diet: remove anger, regret, resentment, guilt, blame and worry. Then watch your health, and life, improve.

Charles F. Glassman

GET MOVING

Whenever you exercise, your body releases endorphins – the feel-good hormone. When you're feeling anxious and low going to the gym could be the last thing on your mind, but getting your body moving will have instant benefits. Taking time out to exercise is a great way to free your mind from your stresses, helping you feel calmer and clearer-headed. Not only are you physically removing yourself from your work or home situation, you are also giving yourself the head space to think things through from a different perspective.

The key is to enjoy whichever exercise you choose. If you don't like to run, try going for a brisk walk. Or if you find it too hard to motivate yourself at the gym, choose an exercise class or group sport instead. Current guidelines suggest exercising for 30 minutes five times a week. Schedule your exercise as you would a work meeting or social engagement because the likelihood is that, even if you don't fancy exercising at the time, you'll be really glad you did afterwards.

**For fast-acting relief,
try slowing down.**

Lily Tomlin

MAKE MOVING FUN

If, for whatever reason, you have negative associations around traditional forms of exercise, try seeking out something new, preferably outdoors where you can breathe fresh air. Look into wild swimming where you can dive into lakes or rivers around the country, water sports classes, hiking clubs or stand-up paddleboarding as great ways to get out into nature – and about as far away from a sweaty gym as possible.

TRY YOGA

Many people underestimate the power of the ancient practice of yoga. Yoga is ideal for calming an anxious mind, working on your breathing and helping you connect with your body. Movements are slow and precise, with a surprising amount of strength and control required, so you will soon find yourself so completely focused on your body and your breath that there is no space for your worries – at least for a short amount of time. You may find that you can transfer some of the breathing practices to your everyday life, so when your stress and anxiety begin to feel overwhelming your yoga training can kick in to help you pause and take some time out.

If you can't find a yoga class near you, there are plenty of lessons and courses to be found on YouTube. There are many different forms of yoga so don't give up if you don't get on with it the first time.

INSTEAD OF
WORRYING ABOUT
WHAT YOU CANNOT
CONTROL, SHIFT
YOUR ENERGY
TO WHAT YOU
CAN CREATE.

Roy Bennett

For me, inactivity is the enemy.

Matt Lucas

Be a
Team Player

Recent research has
shown that being part of
a sports team is not only
good for your physical
health, but it will also help
you feel happier and be
more successful too. As
well as exercising often
you will enjoy regular
social interaction, which
will boost your well-being.
As part of a team you
will feel more fulfilled and

supported and you'll be amazed how the benefits touch every aspect of your life. Forget being picked last in the playground at school – you can choose anything from football or netball to hockey or even Ultimate Frisbee. You'll make new friends, have a fresh support system and will be part of a club. You won't know what you're missing until you try it.

IF YOU WANT TO
CONQUER THE
ANXIETY OF LIFE,
LIVE IN THE MOMENT,
LIVE IN THE BREATH.

AMIT RAY

**Sometimes your joy
is the source of your
smile, but sometimes
your smile can be the
source of your joy.**

Thích Nhất Hạnh

WRITE YOURSELF CALM

Think of three things that went well today. Perhaps you caught the bus on time or a co-worker bought you a coffee. Make a note of why these things happened. It could be because your co-worker noticed how hard you were working, or you set your alarm for 30 minutes earlier which gave you enough time to get ready without rushing. Reflect on the good that's happening in your life right now and feel grateful for the small things.

FOLKS ARE ABOUT
AS HAPPY AS THEY
MAKE UP THEIR
MINDS TO BE.

Anonymous

TAKE A BREATH

One of the most effective ways to take control of your anxiety is to calm your breathing. The more you notice when your breathing starts to become fast and shallow, and the more you practise quality breathing, the easier it will become to soothe anxious thoughts. Start by sitting comfortably in a chair and close your eyes. As you take a breath in, focus on breathing through your nostrils, but try not to force it.

Really focus on how the air enters and leaves your nostrils. Next, place one hand on your chest and the other just below your ribcage. This time, as you breathe in, count to four. Hold your breath for three seconds and count to four as you exhale. Repeat this 4–3–4 pattern and try to focus only on your breathing (the counting should help with this). Try to breathe this way for a few minutes. It may feel awkward at first but taking the time to do some quality breathing will soon become an important part of your daily routine.

LIFE IS A BALANCE
OF HOLDING ON
AND LETTING GO.

Rumi

**To avoid criticism:
do nothing, say nothing,
be nothing.**

Elbert Hubbard

Spring Clean Your Sleep

Falling asleep when your mind won't stop racing is almost impossible, but there are some techniques you can adopt to help ease your passage into the dream world. Firstly, turn off all screens including smartphones, tablets and the TV at least an hour before you go to bed as they have been proved to interfere with the production of melatonin, the sleep hormone. Try to only use your bedroom for sleep and sex. Don't use it as a work base because you will find it harder to switch off from work-related stress. Cut out caffeine after 2 p.m. (yes, really!), and don't do vigorous exercise just before you want to go to bed, as your adrenaline levels will be high. Certain foods, eaten an hour or two before bedtime, such as almonds, turkey or chamomile tea can also help soothe you before you lie down. If you are really struggling to sleep, try reading a good book, focusing on your breathing or listening to a meditation app or podcast.

Sometimes the most important thing in a whole day is the rest we take between two deep breaths.

Etty Hillesum

Nothing can bring you peace but yourself.

Ralph Waldo Emerson

PRACTISE SELF-CARE

If you're feeling overwhelmed, don't be afraid to take a break. You won't offend good friends if you turn down an invitation because you need to take some time to get your anxiety under control. If you're worried about upsetting anyone, offer to do something different with them. It might be a walk in the park or a cup of coffee, instead of cocktails in a crowded bar. It's okay to put your needs first.

Real freedom is saying "no" without giving a reason.

Amit Kalantri

Find Your Happy Place

When you feel your anxiety taking control, shut your eyes if it's safe to do so (not if you're driving or walking) and take yourself to a happy place. Try to conjure a happy memory from your childhood or a beautiful beach you visited on holiday. It can be anything or anywhere, but it must be a place where you felt safe and calm.

Think about every element of your special place: what are the sounds and smells that you remember? Can you feel the sand beneath your toes and taste the salt of the sea on your tongue? Remember how calm and positive you felt when you were there. When you open your eyes, try to hold on to some of those feelings and let the positive glow wash away your anxious thoughts.

EVERY TIME YOU
ARE TEMPTED TO
REACT IN THE SAME
OLD WAY, ASK IF
YOU WANT TO BE
A PRISONER OF THE
PAST OR A PIONEER
OF THE FUTURE.

DEEPAK CHOPRA

More compassion, less judgment. More blessed, less stressed.

Roy T. Bennett

CLEAR YOUR CLUTTER

A messy room has more of an impact than you may realize. Messy floors and surfaces will remind you of tasks left undone, and clutter makes it hard for you to switch off mentally and physically – especially if you can never find what you need. Tackle the problem room by room and take time to think about the items you want to keep and those you can let go. Having a clear-out can be therapeutic and it will result in a calmer living space.

NEVER LET LIFE'S HARDSHIPS DISTURB YOU... NO ONE CAN AVOID PROBLEMS, NOT EVEN SAINTS OR SAGES.

Nichiren

Does Your Anxiety Have a Purpose?

Believe it or not some negative thoughts can be useful. It can feel slightly strange to think that something that causes us so much pain and distress could be helpful, but often negative or anxious thoughts are a way of your brain trying to warn or protect you.

Perhaps your anxious thoughts are reminding

you to stay physically safe or not to upset someone else with your words. It could be a sign you're working too hard and not taking enough time to relax and recover from a stressful week. Or if family or friends are making you feel unsettled, it might be time to politely refuse the next invitation to lunch. Instead of trying to crush your anxious thoughts, take some time to decode them in case they are telling you something important.

THERE IS SOMETHING
WONDERFULLY BOLD
AND LIBERATING
ABOUT SAYING
YES TO OUR ENTIRE
IMPERFECT AND
MESSY LIFE.

TARA BRACH

Nothing can harm you as much as your own thoughts unguarded.

Buddha

OUR WOUNDS
ARE OFTEN THE
OPENINGS INTO THE
MOST BEAUTIFUL
PART OF US.

David Richo

REWIRE YOUR BRAIN

Using positive affirmations is recognized as a way of calming an overly anxious and negative mind and reprogramming your subconscious to be more positive. You can use phrases such as, "I believe in, trust and have confidence in myself" or "I look for humour and fun in most situations". These might not feel true at first, but the more you repeat them in your head, the more they will start to feel possible and soon become reality.

Meditation
practice isn't about
trying to throw ourselves
away and become
something better. It's
about befriending who
we are already.

Pema Chödrön

**Mindfulness isn't difficult.
We just need to
remember to do it.**

Sharon Salzberg

EMBRACE MINDFULNESS

Anxiety is often rooted in future events and what *might* happen. Mindfulness is the absolute opposite of this, encouraging you to live in the moment and helping to ground your awareness of what is happening in the present. Try this simple exercise to practise mindfulness as you eat: notice the colours on your plate, the smell of your meal, the feel of your knife slicing through the food, and the feeling and texture in your mouth as you taste and chew. Put your knife and fork down after each bite and stop to appreciate the flavours. Simply slowing down and living in the moment will alleviate your anxiety as there will be no space for it in your mindful mind. Like any skill, it will take practice to master, but spending some time on mindfulness could free you from your negative thought patterns and boost your self-esteem.

Worry never robs tomorrow of its sorrow, it only saps today of its joy.

Leo Buscaglia

THE SOCIAL MINEFIELD

While social media is a great way of keeping in touch with friends and family, there is no getting away from the fact it can have a really negative effect on your mental health. Seeing everyone else seemingly having fun can lead you to feel as though you are missing out, and you can feel under pressure to present a perfect version of your life that may be far from the truth. Don't be afraid to take a step back if you need to.

WE COMPARE OUR
BEHIND-THE-SCENES
WITH EVERYONE ELSE'S
HIGHLIGHT REEL.

Steven Furtick

SOCIAL MEDIA TIME OUT

Think about taking some time out from your social media accounts. There's a good chance that no one will even notice. You don't need to make a big announcement, although you might feel you want to. Simply turn off notifications and delete the apps from your phone to remove temptation. You'll find yourself with more free time to focus on yourself and your own well-being, rather than being distracted by hundreds of updates.

You can't always control what goes on outside. But you can always control what goes on inside.

Wayne Dyer

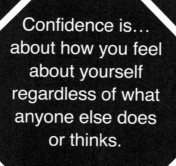

Confidence is…
about how you feel
about yourself
regardless of what
anyone else does
or thinks.

Jen Sincero

STREAMLINE YOUR ACCOUNTS

Over the years you've probably followed or befriended hundreds of people online who are not part of your life any more. Take some time to look at your social media accounts and unfollow or block anyone who is no longer relevant or whose posts don't bring you happiness. Maybe a particular person's posts trigger your anxiety, or you just no longer want them as part of your life. If unfollowing someone or blocking them feels too extreme, try muting their account for a while.

LET US BE GRATEFUL
TO PEOPLE WHO
MAKE US HAPPY; THEY
ARE THE CHARMING
GARDENERS WHO
MAKE OUR SOULS
BLOSSOM.

Marcel Proust

No one can make you feel inferior without your consent.

Eleanor Roosevelt

Act the way that
you want to feel.

Gretchen Rubin

DETOX YOUR FRIENDSHIP GROUP

Treat your real-life friends the same way you do your online ones: if they make you feel good about yourself, are fun to be with and add something to your life, then keep them around. If they don't tick any of those boxes, ask yourself why you are still friends with them. There is no point spending time with someone who makes you feel unhappy and anxious. You don't always need to have a big break up – quietly phasing them out may work.

A sweet friendship
refreshes the soul

Proverbs 27:9

Family Ties

You can't choose your family, but you can communicate clearly with them. If you live with your family, they may already be aware of your struggles with anxiety, but if you live apart there is a good chance they don't know what is going on in your life. Share your fears and worries with them. Siblings and parents have known you all your life and they may have some insight as to why you're feeling this way or if there is a family history of anxiety. Of course, your family may be a key source of your anxiety, in which case don't be afraid to take some time away from them for a while. Talking to a therapist may also help if you have family issues that are feeding into your anxiety.

Life will test you, but remember this: when you walk up a mountain, your legs get stronger.

Anonymous

The way you tell your story to yourself matters.

Amy Cuddy

RELATIONSHIP MOT

Living with anxiety can put a lot of strain on a relationship and however supportive your partner tries to be they might not always get it right. Take some time to tell them how much you appreciate their support, but also explain how you're feeling and let them know the ways they can help you. Perhaps you need them to remind you to go out for a walk when you're feeling stressed, or you need to be left alone to practise your breathing exercises. Remember, your partner may love you, but they are not a mind reader. Tell them what you need and they can try to give it to you. If your partner is struggling to support you, then you may need to look for help elsewhere. This could be from a close friend or a professional.

Sometimes crying or laughing are the only options left, and laughing feels better right now.

Veronica Roth

If you can't make it better, you can laugh at it.

Erma Bombeck

LAUGH OUT LOUD

Laughter really is the best medicine, mainly because it serves as a good distraction from those things that are causing you stress. It can also give you a different perspective on events that you are finding stressful, helping you to see them as challenges instead. By looking at events with a sense of humour you can see testing times as a funny story to tell your friends later rather than a stressful occasion. Laughter is a social thing and is infectious, so surround yourself with people who like a laugh. And don't worry if you're not feeling funny; if you fake a smile or laugh, you still get some of the benefits and it will probably result in real mirth anyway. So, watch a comedy on TV or plug in to a humorous podcast and get your giggle on.

FILL YOUR GLASS

It isn't always easy to look on the bright side of life, but sometimes making yourself think of the positives will help you feel better. Create a list of things you are grateful for in your life. Maybe you have good health or a supportive family or your career is going really well. It could be something as simple as living near a beautiful river or park that you enjoy walking in. If you're struggling, ask a friend to help come up with ideas.

Turn your face to the sun and the shadows fall behind you.

Maori proverb

Workplace Worries

Your job can be one of the main sources of stress and anxiety in your life. You may have a demanding boss, unhelpful work colleagues or an unrealistic workload – whatever it is, there are things you can do to help make your work life more pleasant. The first step is to find out exactly what is stressing you out. Write a list of all the things that are worrying you about work – seeing it in black and white will help you understand where your anxiety is coming from. Then break down the list and think about what can be done to address each problem. You'll feel a lot less overwhelmed and you can work on an action plan. Hopefully soon you won't dread Monday mornings quite so much.

THE SUN HIMSELF
IS WEAK WHEN HE
FIRST RISES AND
GATHERS STRENGTH
AND COURAGE AS
THE DAY GETS ON.

CHARLES DICKENS

What we see depends mainly on what we look for.

John Lubbock

YOU
DESERVE IT

You know the feeling when you're scared everyone will find out that you're no good at your job and you've just been "getting away with it" all this time? Well, guess what? Lots of other people feel this way too. The good news is that it is almost definitely not the case. If you need some cold hard proof, make a list of all the things you've achieved in your career – this could be anything from winning a big contract to never missing a deadline. Ask a work colleague or friend who knows you well to come up with some of your best qualities too. Chances are you are doing a great job, and it will be a good confidence boost to reassure yourself of that fact.

Successful people keep moving. They make mistakes, but they don't quit.

Conrad Hilton

Always be a first-rate version of yourself, instead of a second-rate version of somebody else.

Judy Garland

Negativity at Work

Unfortunately, sometimes you might have to deal with someone in your workplace who doesn't make you feel good about yourself. It might not always be obvious how or why they are making you feel this way. Maybe they are putting you down in front of your boss or leaving you out of office socials. It can sometimes feel like you're imagining it or overreacting.

so talk to work colleagues to see if they've noticed anything. If it is really affecting your performance at work, speak to your line manager or HR department.

IF SOMETHING IS WRONG, FIX IT IF YOU CAN. BUT TRAIN YOURSELF NOT TO WORRY: WORRY FIXES NOTHING.

Ernest Hemingway

Smile, breathe, and go slowly.

Thích Nhất Hạnh

Take Control of Your Work

It can sometimes feel like you are drowning in work and deadlines, and that there is no way out. Don't let your workload overwhelm you. If you need to, ask for help and explain to your line manager that you are struggling. Try to offer your own solution to the problem too. Perhaps you could ask for a deadline extension for one of your projects or a colleague could offer you some support. Make sure you flag up any problems in plenty of time. Try to look at your methods of working, too: is there anything you could do to prevent yourself from getting so overwhelmed, such as managing your workflow, turning down meeting requests or leaving your emails until a certain point in the day?

FEELINGS ARE MUCH
LIKE WAVES; WE
CAN'T STOP THEM
FROM COMING
BUT WE CAN
CHOOSE WHICH
ONES TO SURF.

JONATAN MÅRTENSSON

QUIT IF YOU NEED TO

Sometimes the signs are so bright they could be flashing in neon above your head. If your work is severely affecting your mental health, it could be time to find a job that is a better fit. This doesn't mean you should quit every time you need to give a tricky presentation or lead an important project. Instead, try asking for a mentor or see if there is a training course that could help. But if you've tried everything and you know it will never get any better, it's probably time to go.

FIX YOUR FINANCES

Nothing keeps you up at night and increases anxiety like an unauthorized overdraft and a steadily increasing credit card bill. Money and mental health go hand in hand, so one can easily have an effect on the other. Not having enough money to pay your bills will cause your anxiety levels to rocket, but feeling anxious and struggling with your mood can also cause you to spend more than you can afford. The first thing you need to do is face up to your money worries. Stop ignoring your bills and get everything all in one place – a spreadsheet is a great way to organize your income and outgoings or there are plenty of apps to help you budget. There are lots of financial helplines to give you advice, but don't just hope it will all go away, because it won't – you need to take control of your finances.

OUR INCOMES
ARE LIKE OUR SHOES;
IF TOO SMALL, THEY
GALL AND PINCH US;
BUT IF TOO LARGE,
THEY CAUSE US TO
STUMBLE AND TO TRIP.

John Locke

That man is rich whose pleasures are the cheapest.

Henry David Thoreau

Sensible Spending

Managing your money is all about balancing your income with your outgoings. While it might be hard to earn additional money, you can certainly try to reduce what you spend. This doesn't mean you need to become a hermit, but some sensible budgeting and planning should help.

  Keep a note of how much you spend over the course of a month and see where you can make savings. Check your utility bills and see if you can swap to cheaper providers, take a packed lunch to work instead of buying it in a café and offer to cook your friends dinner instead of going out to eat. Buy second-hand clothes instead of new and take public transport instead of taxis. Perhaps you can sell some of your belongings on eBay or take on some overtime at work to make some quick extra cash. Explain to friends that you might have to miss a couple of social events as you're trying to get your spending back on track. You'll soon find getting your finances under control will help soothe your anxiety in all areas of life.

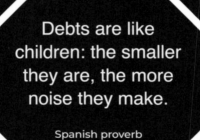

Debts are like children: the smaller they are, the more noise they make.

Spanish proverb

Maybe you have to know the darkness before you can appreciate the light.

Madeleine L'Engle

Dealing
with Debt

If you do have serious
debts, you will need to
get professional help. The
first step is to contact
a debt consolidation
firm, which can help you
contact everyone you owe
money to and work out
a repayment plan. Don't
be tempted by "payday"
loans, which are short
term and high interest;
they may seem like a good

solution but will actually add to the problem. Make sure you are honest about how much you owe, open all your previously ignored bills and take a look at why you have been spending so much. Confide in friends and family for support. Remember, lots of people get into debt and it is nothing to be ashamed of. The first and hardest step is reaching out for help, but you will never regret dealing with your debt.

Striving for excellence motivates you; striving for perfection is demoralizing.

Harriet Braiker

Debt is like any other trap: easy enough to get into, but hard enough to get out of.

Josh Billings

DON'T SEEK PERFECTION

If you hold yourself to impossibly high standards, be it in your work or your home life, you will soon find yourself struggling with anxiety. No one is perfect so the sooner you let go of that idea the better. Start by thinking about why you feel the need to be perfect and what's behind that urge. See if you can identify areas where you already feel "good enough". Now try to replicate that in other areas of your life where you are holding yourself to impossible standards. See if you can allow yourself to be imperfect and happy, as opposed to striving for perfection. Look to other people you admire and try to see their flaws as well as their positive traits. You can still be successful and happy without being perfect – and who needs to be perfect? Happiness is being the person you are and not living up to an unachievable standard of perfection.

WE ARE PERFECT IN OUR IMPERFECTION.

MEGAN McCAFFERTY

Instead of "Let it go", we should probably say "Let it be".

Jon Kabat-Zinn

FACE YOUR FEARS

It can be tempting to avoid scenarios that cause you anxiety, but this can sometimes make things worse. Establish whether you're taking time out to recuperate or if you're hiding from the problem. Often it is better to confront a situation and work through your fears. It might not be as bad as you think, plus you will learn some valuable coping skills in the process.

I know for sure that what we dwell on is what we become.

Oprah Winfrey

You are Unique

It is all too easy to compare yourself with the most successful of your friends, whether they are doing amazingly at work or have a seemingly perfect relationship and unshakable confidence. But regardless of whether this is true or not, stop comparing yourself with others. Everyone has their own life to live and comparison only leads to unhappiness. Success and happiness can come in many forms and what works for one person might not be right for another. Look at your own achievements and appreciate how far you've come. Focus on your needs and happiness and work out what it is you need to keep yourself moving forward toward your goals, whatever they may be.

WHEN WE DO THE BEST
WE CAN, WE NEVER
KNOW WHAT MIRACLE
IS WROUGHT IN OUR
LIFE, OR IN THE LIFE
OF ANOTHER.

Helen Keller

**Whatever you do
you have to keep
moving forward.**

Martin Luther King Jr

DOING GOOD DOES YOU GOOD

You might feel as though you don't have the capacity to help anyone else, but actually volunteering or helping someone can make you feel better. Carrying out an act of kindness will help put your worries in perspective, make you feel more connected to other people and help you feel less stressed, as well as giving your self-esteem a boost. Just be sure to leave some time for yourself, too!

TRY TO BE A RAINBOW
IN SOMEONE'S CLOUD.

Maya Angelou

Find a Therapy for You

You don't have to deal with your anxiety alone – there are plenty of therapies designed to ease your worries and support you. One of the best tools is learning CBT (cognitive behavioural therapy), which addresses negative thought patterns and behaviours. It works on the premise that if you can change the way you think about things you can change the way you feel about them. There are books on CBT but often working with a specialist is most successful.

Or perhaps you might respond to hypnotherapy, where a therapist will help you to face your fears and look at them in a different way. You may need to try a variety of therapies to find the one that works for you.

Just when the caterpillar thought the world was ending, she became a butterfly.

Barbara Haines Howett

As soon as you trust yourself, you will know how to live.

Johann Wolfgang von Goethe

IT'S NOT YOU

It is all too easy to take to heart the things that happen to you, both good and bad. Maybe you've been made redundant or a relationship has ended. That doesn't mean you were a terrible partner or useless at your job; it just means that right now your circumstances have changed. Try not to let yourself be defined by a single event. You are not terrible at your job or doomed to be single forever just because something hasn't worked out this time. Don't let other people define your feelings, but instead learn to limit their effect on you. Have some phrases to hand to deal with negative comments, such as: "Thanks for your opinion, but I don't see it that way" or "That is one way of looking at things". By pushing away their negativity you will also find it easier to shut down your own negative inner voice and replace it with a more positive one, building up your self-esteem in the process.

Running away from your problems is a race you'll never win. Face them head-on, knowing there will be brighter days.

Anonymous

YOU ARE BRAVER
THAN YOU BELIEVE,
STRONGER THAN YOU
SEEM AND SMARTER
THAN YOU THINK.

A. A. MILNE

One Step at a Time

Overcoming anxiety is not easily done, but whether you've lived with it for a lifetime or have recently started suffering, there is a way through. Take small steps every day toward positive thinking. Challenge the negative thoughts you have and try to rationalize them with truth. Speak to someone you can trust, such as a friend or family member, and if you are really struggling speak to a medical professional or call an emergency

If you're interested in finding
out more about our books,
find us on Facebook at
Summersdale Publishers
and follow us on Twitter
at **@Summersdale**.

www.summersdale.com

Image credits

pp.4, 12, 27, 31, 39, 44, 58, 69, 74, 81, 82, 89, 91, 93, 95, 132, 143, 149 © Vanzyst/Shutterstock.com

pp.9, 21, 24, 29, 48, 53, 63, 83, 94, 97, 113, 129, 133, 147 © Plasteed/Shutterstock.com helpline if you're worried you can't cope with your feelings. You are on a journey to calm your mind and control your anxiety. It won't be easy, but you can do it: just take one small step at a time and look forward to your new, calm, normal.